Ahoi Ashtami Vrat

AF663740

Illustrations: Sujata Saha

Publisher: DivineBharat

© 2025 DivineBharat

Illustrations: Sujata Saha

All rights reserved. No part of this book, whether in whole or in part, may be reproduced, printed, digitized, or distributed in any form without prior written permission from the author or publisher.

ISBN 978-93-343-8907-4

Publisher: DivineBharat

Website: www.divinebharat.co

Table of Contents

1. **Introduction**
    - Baina in Ahoi Ashtami Vrat
    - Radhakund Snan – Complete Procedure
2. **Puja Materials**
3. **Puja Preparation**
4. **Puja Procedure**
    - Sankalp Vidhi (Vow-taking ritual)
    - Ganesh Puja
    - Ahoi Mata Puja
    - Special Mala Method
    - Katha
    - Arghya Offering and Breaking the Fast
    - Giving Baina
    - Conclusion of Puja
5. **Special Traditions**
    - Radhakund Snan
    - Special Use of Prasad
6. **Vrat Stories**
    - Ganesh Vrat Katha
    - Ahoi Ashtami Vrat Katha
7. **Aarti**
    - Shri Ganesh Ji Aarti
    - Ahoi Mata Aarti

Introduction

Ahoi Ashtami Vrat is one of the major and traditional festivals in Hinduism, observed by mothers with devotion and faith for the long life, prosperity, and well-being of their children. In ancient times, this fast was especially observed for the welfare of sons, but in modern times, mothers keep it for the well-being of all their children — both sons and daughters.

This fast is observed about eight days before Diwali, on the Ashtami (eighth day) of the Krishna Paksha. According to the Purnimant calendar followed in North India, it falls in the month of Kartik, whereas in Gujarat, Maharashtra, and other southern states that follow the Amanta calendar, it falls in the month of Ashwin. Although the name of the month differs in these calendars, the date and the festival day remain the same everywhere.

Ahoi Ashtami is also known as Ahoi Aathe because it is celebrated on the Ashtami tithi. On this day, Ahoi Mata is worshipped, who is considered the protector and benefactor of children. In some regions, Ahoi Mata is regarded as a form of Goddess Lakshmi.

The fast begins in the morning with a ritual bath, followed by taking a vow (sankalp) to observe a waterless fast for the well-being of one's children. After fasting the whole day, the vrat is broken in the evening during godhuli bela (dusk) after sighting the stars. In some traditions, the fast is concluded after moonrise, but since the moon rises quite late on this day, it becomes difficult to follow this practice.

For the puja, an image of Ahoi Mata is usually drawn on the wall using red ochre (geru) or embroidered/printed on a cloth and hung for worship. The image traditionally has eight corners or boxes, symbolizing the Ashtami tithi. It also depicts Ahoi Mata along with a tiger and small children. Items such as a kalash (sacred pot), karwa (water vessel), sarai sticks or cotton wicks, wheat grains, halwa, poori, and pooa hold special significance in the rituals.

A popular folk tale is associated with Ahoi Ashtami, in which a merchant's wife accidentally kills a tiger cub and consequently suffers the loss of her children. Later, by worshipping and observing the vrat of Ahoi Mata, her sin is absolved, and she is blessed with children again. This story symbolizes motherly devotion, repentance, and the deep love for one's children.

Ahoi Ashtami Vrat is not merely a religious ritual but a living celebration of a mother's compassion, love, and sacrifice — a tradition that has been passed down through generations in Indian culture, carrying forward the timeless prayer for the welfare of children.

Baina in Ahoi Ashtami Vrat

The word "Baina" refers to a decorated plate or tray containing special items arranged for the observance of a vow (vrat) or for worship.

- It is an auspicious combination of clothes, adornment items, sweets, fruits, and other pooja materials.
- The tradition of giving Baina is associated with blessings and good wishes, intended to ensure the continued happiness and prosperity of the household.

In the Ahoi Vrat, Baina is usually given to the mother-in-law (saas) or elder sister-in-law (jethani). It may include—

1. Pooja Thali – containing roli (red vermilion powder), rice, halwa, poori, fruits, sweets, sindoor (vermilion), comb, bangles, bindis, cloth, etc.
2. Coconut – often considered an essential element of worship.
3. Lota filled with water – decorated with roli and rice.
4. Sweets or festive dishes – such as halwa-poori, mathri, etc.

Radhakund Snan

Mythological Background and Glory

- Radhakund is the sacred place where Lord Shri Krishna and Radharani bathed, establishing its divine sanctity. According to the legend, Radharani dug this pond with her bracelet—hence it is also called *"Kangan Kund."* In accordance with Radharani's wish, Shri Krishna granted the boon that whoever bathes here on this day will be blessed with a son.

- Ahoi Ashtami, observed on the Krishna Paksha Ashtami of the Kartik month, holds special significance for bathing in Radhakund—this is considered the most auspicious opportunity for attaining the blessing of children.

Bathing Procedure

1. **Observe a Nirjala Vrat** – Most couples fast without consuming food or water, as a vow of dedication.
2. **Begin the bath at midnight (12 a.m.)** – Enter the river or pond in artificial darkness, and bathe with focus and devotion.
3. **Offer sincere prayers** – Pray to Radharani for the fulfillment of desires, especially for the blessing of children.
4. **Required worship materials:**
   - *Kushmanda* (white pumpkin/ash gourd), decorated with a red cloth and offered to Radharani.
   - Prasad is offered at the kund either before or after the bath.
5. **Devotee gatherings and vows** – A large number of married women, couples, and devotees participate in this sacred bath; many take three dips to express their faith.
6. **Post-bath tradition** – After the bath, devotees circumambulate Govardhan Hill, and if blessed with a child, they return to this place to express their gratitude.

Puja Materials

1. Picture or calendar of Ahoi Mata (depicting Ahoi Mata, Sei, Surya, Lord Ganesha, and Goddess Lakshmi).
2. Geru (red ochre) and lime (if making a drawing of Ahoi Mata on the wall or floor).
3. Idol or picture of Lord Ganesha (if installing separately).
4. Two ghat / earthen pots (kalash) — one with a karva placed on top.
5. Grains (wheat, rice) or water for filling the pots.
6. Mauli (sacred red thread).
7. Saptadhanya (seven types of grains, especially seven wheat grains).
8. Flowers, roli (vermilion), rice, turmeric, akshat (unbroken rice grains).
9. Incense sticks, lamp, ghee/oil.
10. Prasad — puris, jaggery/sugar balls, halwa or gulgule, laddus, etc.
11. Baina (sari/bangles/sindoor/mehndi/ coin, etc.).
12. Silver Ahoi (Syau) — if it is the family tradition.
13. Kushmanda (white ash gourd) — especially for Radhakund Snan.

Auspicious Time for Puja

- **Most auspicious time: Immediately after sunset, during the evening (*Sandhya*) period.**
- **Breaking the fast: After sighting the stars or at moonrise, according to family tradition.**

Puja Preparations

- Take the ***sankalp*** (ritual vow) in the morning or just before beginning the puja.
- Observe the fast for the entire day — either ***nirjala*** (without food and water) **or with fruits**, depending on your capacity.
- Clean the puja area and spread a sanctified seat (***asana***).
- Place the picture of Ahoi Mata on the wall or on a low wooden platform (*paata*).
- If drawing the picture, make Ahoi Mata, Sei, and the seven sons using geru (red ochre) and lime.

Puja Method – Sankalp (Vow)

On the day of Ahoi Vrat, the *sankalp* (ritual vow) is taken in the morning or just before starting the puja. Traditionally, this is done while sitting on a *kusha* grass seat, holding water, rice, and flowers in the hand.

After bathing and wearing clean clothes, prepare the puja place. Sit on a seat made of *kusha* grass or a clean cloth. Hold rice (*akshat*), flowers, and water in one hand. Clearly recite your *gotra* (lineage), name, place, date, the name of the vrat, and its purpose. Finally, pour the water onto the ground — this is considered the confirmation of the *sankalp*.

Sankalp Statement:

"I, (your name), am observing the Ahoi Mata Vrat today (mention date and place). I undertake this vrat for the long life, good health, and prosperity of my children. I will observe it in the nirjala form (without food and water). This vrat will be completed only after offering arghya to the stars or the moon after sunset."

Om Parvatipriyanandanaya Namah I

Om Umadevyai Namah I

Ganesh Puja

1. Offer *roli* (red sacred powder) and *akshat* (unbroken rice) to Lord Ganesha.
2. Light a lamp and pray to Lord Ganesha to remove all obstacles from the worship.

Ahoi Mata Puja

1. Offer *roli*, *akshat*, and flowers to Ahoi Mata, Sei, Surya, Lakshmi, and Ganesha.
2. Apply *tilak* to your children and tie *kalawa* (sacred red-yellow thread) on their wrists.
3. Drape a *chunari* (decorative scarf) over Ahoi Mata's image/idol and offer a garland.
4. Make a *tilak* and *swastika* symbol on the two *ghar/handis* (earthen pots), and offer rice.

Special Mala Ritual

- Replace the thread in Ahoi Mata's garland.
- Wear this garland around your neck while listening to the *katha*, keep it on until the fast is broken, then place it on the *do-ghar* (two earthen pots).

Listening to the Katha

- Listen to the story (*katha*) of Ahoi Mata — a tale that blesses children with long life and brings the joy of progeny.
- After this, the story of Lord Ganesha is also heard.
- During the katha, hold seven grains of wheat/rice and a little *dhoop* (incense) or *jaware* (sprouted barley) in your hands.

Arghya and Breaking the Fast

1. At night, see the stars or the moon.
2. Put the wheat/rice from the katha into the water of the *karwa* or *kalash*.
3. Offer this water as *arghya* (libation) while praying.
4. Break the fast and partake of the *prasad*.

Giving Baina

- After the puja, give *baina* (offering) — such as a sari, bangles, sindoor, mehendi, or a coin — to your mother-in-law, elder sister-in-law (*jethani*), sister-in-law (*nanad*), or any elder woman.

- If there is no such person at home, give it to a woman in the temple or a neighbor.

Conclusion of the Puja

- Remove the image of Ahoi Mata and the *do-ghar* (two earthen pots) only on *Chhoti Diwali*.
- Use the water from the *do-ghar* for bathing the children and sprinkling around the house.

Special Traditions

- **Radhakund Snan:** For the blessing of children, couples take a holy bath at midnight during the *nishita kaal* and offer *kushmanda* (pumpkin) in the sacred pond.
- **Throwing Pooris:** In some places, *pooris* from the prasad are thrown behind oneself; children pick them up and eat them — this is considered a symbol of happiness and prosperity.

Ganesh Vrat Katha

Ek bar Mata Parvati ne Bhagwan Shiv se kaha – "He Swami! Main chahti hoon ki aap mujhe aisa vrat batayen jisse santan sukh prapt ho aur santan lambi ayu wali ho."

Tab Bhagwan Shiv ne kaha – "He Parvati! Sabhi vraton me Ganesh Vrat shreshth hai. Ise karne se vrati ko santan sukh aur sabhi karyon me safalta milti hai. Is vrat me Ganeshji ki puja karke, dhoop-deep se aradhana karni chahiye aur sankalp lekar poore din nirjal rehna chahiye."

Bhagwan Shiv ne Ganesh Vrat ki mahima suna kar yah bhi kaha ki jo stri Ahoi Ashtami ke din Ganesh Vrat karti hai, uski santan ki sabhi badhayein samapt ho jati hain.

Ant me katha sunne ke bad vrati mahilayen kahti hain "Ganpati Bappa Morya, Mangal Murti Morya, hamare vrat ko poorn karen, sukh-shanti pradan karen."

Ahoi Ashtami Vrat Katha

Ek maa aur uske saat beton ki katha

Ek samay ki baat hai, ghane jungle ke paas base ek gaon me ek dayalu aur dharmaparayan mahila rehti thi. Uske saat bete the. Kartik maas me, Diwali se kuch din pehle, us mahila ne Diwali ke liye apne ghar ki marammat aur sajawat karne ka faisla kiya. Apne ghar ki marammat ke liye, vah jungle se mitti lane gayi. Jungle me mitti khodte samay, jis kudal se vah mitti khod rahi thi, usse galti se kuch chhote hathi ke bachche mare gaye.

Un masoom suaron ke saath jo hua, uske liye vah khud ko dukhi, doshi aur zimmedar mahsus kar rahi thi.

Is ghatna ke ek varsh ke bheetar, us mahila ke sabhi saat bete gayab ho gaye aur unhen graminon ne mrut maan liya. Graminon ne anuman lagaya ki uske beton ko jungle ke kuch jangli janwaron ne maar diya hoga. Mahila bahut udaas thi aur usne saare durbhagya ko apne dwara shavak ki akasmik mrutyu se joda. Ek din, usne gaon ki ek vruddh mahila ko apni vyatha sunai. Usne is ghatna ke baare me bataya ki kaise usne galti se shavak ko maarne ka paap kiya tha. Vruddh mahila ne mahila ko salah di ki apne paap ke prayashchit ke liye, use Devi Parvati ke avataar Devi Ahoi Bhagwati se suar ke bachche ka chehra banakar prarthana karni chahiye. Use Devi

Ahoi ke liye vrat rakhne aur puja karne ka sujhav diya gaya kyonki unhen sabhi jeevit praniyon ki santanon ki rakshak mana jata tha.

Mahila ne Ashtami ke din Devi Ahoi ki puja karne ka nishchay kiya. Jab Ashtami ka din aaya, to mahila ne suar ka chehra banaya aur vrat rakhkar Ahoi Mata ki puja ki. Usne apne kiye paap ka sacche man se pashchatap kiya. Devi Ahoi uski bhakti aur imandari se prasan hui aur uske samne prakat hui aur use uske putron ki dirghayu ka vardaan diya. Sheeghr hi uske saaton putr jeevit ghar laut aaye. Us din se, har varsh Kartik Krishna Ashtami ke din Devi Ahoi Bhagwati ki puja karne ka vidhan ban gaya. Is din mataen apne bachchon ki salamat ke liye prarthana aur vrat rakhti hain.

II Shri Ganesh Ji Aarti II

Jai Ganesh Jai Ganesh, Jai Ganesh
Deva.
Mata Jaki Parvati, Pita Mahadeva.

Ek Dant Dayavant, Char Bhuja Dhari.
Mathe Sindoor Sohe, Moose Ki
Sawari.

Jai Ganesh Jai Ganesh, Jai Ganesh
Deva.
Mata Jaki Parvati, Pita Mahadeva.

Paan Chade Phal Chade, Aur Chade
Meva.
Ladduan Ka Bhog Lage, Sant Karen
Seva.

Jai Ganesh Jai Ganesh, Jai Ganesh
Deva.
Mata Jaki Parvati, Pita Mahadeva.

Andhan Ko Aankh Det, Kodhin Ko
Kaya.
Banjhan Ko Putra Det, Nirdhan Ko
Maya.

Jai Ganesh Jai Ganesh, Jai Ganesh
Deva.
Mata Jaki Parvati, Pita Mahadeva.

'Soor' Shyam Sharan Aaye, Safal
Keeje Seva.
Mata Jaki Parvati, Pita Mahadeva.

Jai Ganesh Jai Ganesh, Jai Ganesh
Deva.
Mata Jaki Parvati, Pita Mahadeva.

Deenan Ki Laj Rakho, Shambhu
Sutkari.
Kamna Ko Poorn Karo, Jaaun
Balihari.

Jai Ganesh Jai Ganesh, Jai Ganesh
Deva.
Mata Jaki Parvati, Pita Mahadeva.

II Aarti Ahoi Mata Ki II

Jai Ahoi Mata.
Tumko Nis Din Dhyavat, Har Vishnu Vidhata.
Om Jai Ahoi Mata.

Brahmani, Rudrani, Kamala, Tu Hi Hai Jagmata.
Surya-Chandrama Dhyavat, Narad Rishi Gata.
Om Jai Ahoi Mata.

Mata Roop Niranjan, Sukh-Sampatti Data.
Jo Koi Tumko Dhyavat, Nit Mangal Pata.
Om Jai Ahoi Mata.

Tu Hi Patal Basanti, Tu Hi Hai Shubhdata.
Karm-Prabhav Prakashak, Jagnidhi Se Trata.
Om Jai Ahoi Mata.

Jis Ghar Tharo Vasa, Vahi Mein Gun Aata.
Kar Na Sake Soi Kar Le, Man Nahin Ghabrata.
Om Jai Ahoi Mata.

Tum Bin Sukh Na Hove, Na Koi Putra Pata.
Khan-Pan Ka Vaibhav, Tum Bin Nahin Aata.
Om Jai Ahoi Mata.

Shubh Gun Sundar Yukta, Kshir Nidhi Jata.
Ratan Chaturdash Toku, Koi Nahin Pata.
Om Jai Ahoi Mata.

Shri Ahoi Maa Ki Aarti, Jo Koi Gata.
Ur Umang Ati Upaje, Paap Utar Jata.
Om Jai Ahoi Mata,
Maiya Jai Ahoi Mata.

9 789334 389074

Printed at Repro India Ltd.